If A Man Die,
Shall He Live Again?

Comforting Words about Heaven
and Life after Death

I0558943

ISBN: 979-8-9905333-4-9

Dr. Tom Sexton

Five Star
CHRISTIAN MINISTRIES

Presented to

_____

_____

on

_____

_____

by

_____

_____

The Lord Jesus said,

"In my Father's house are many mansions: if it were not so, I would have told you. I go to prepare a place for you.

And if I go and prepare a place for you, I will come again, and receive you unto myself; that where I am, there ye may be also."

John 14:2-3

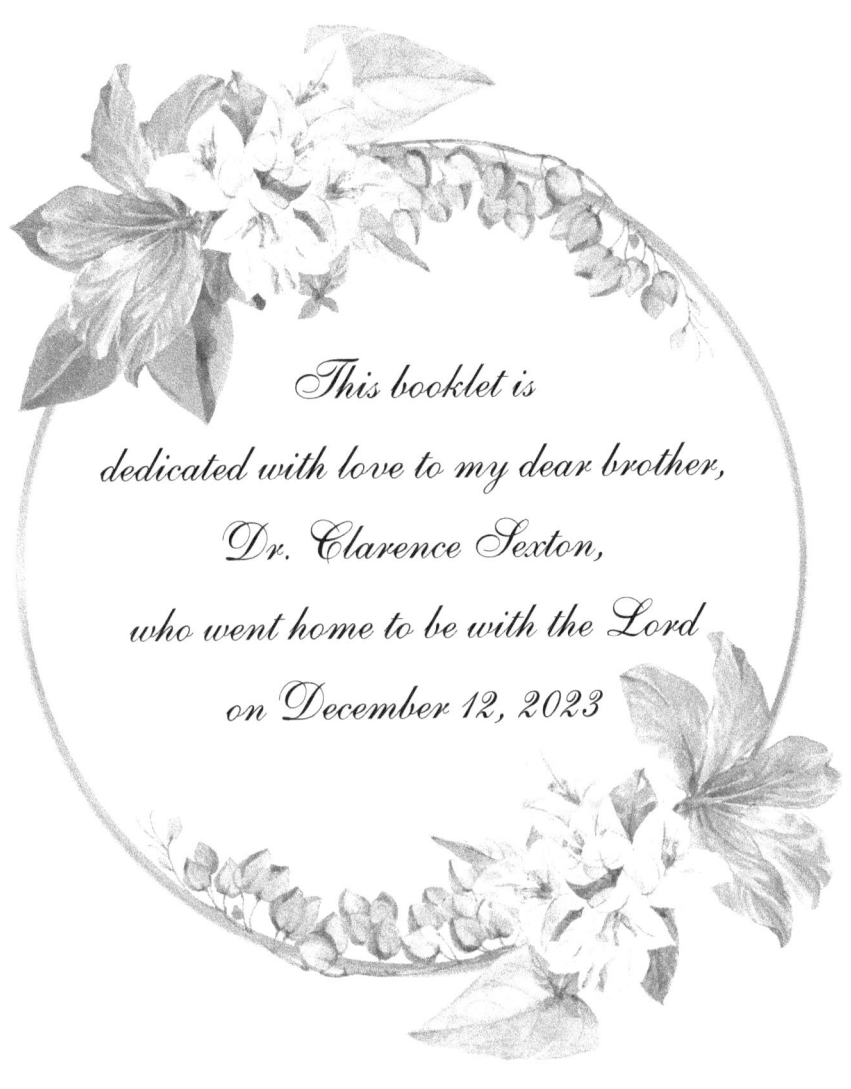

This booklet is
dedicated with love to my dear brother,
Dr. Clarence Sexton,
who went home to be with the Lord
on December 12, 2023

My brother did for me what Andrew did
for his brother,

"He first findeth his own brother...and he
brought him to Jesus."

John 1:41-42

Contents

Introduction

The Bible says, *"It is appointed unto men once to die, but after this the judgment."* Hebrews 9:27

We all have an appointment with death. Some die suddenly and unexpectedly. Some die after a long battle with a disease or illness. Some die of old age; they come to the end of a long life and close their eyes in death. We accept coming to the end of life, and dying old, but the first two are more difficult for us to accept.

People who die suddenly have very little suffering, if any. One moment they are here and the next in Heaven, if they are believers. Their death is easier on them, but harder for others to accept. Too many unanswered questions are left behind. In most cases no plans were made for their death.

People who die from a long battle with illness know how they are going to die; they just do not know when. They do, however, get to finalize their life and bring it to a close. They can prepare others for their impend-

★ ★ ★ ★ ★   1

ing death, and they can prepare to meet God. They can leave behind a final chapter of their life, the way they choose.

It is **important** to know where you are going when you die. It is **more important** to be ready for your death. But, the **most important** is for all those who know you to join you in Heaven.

This book was written to help people with the next chapter of life and to comfort those left behind.

Mans Oldest Question

The question that has been on the hearts and minds of people down through the centuries is this:

"If A Man Die, Shall He Live Again?"

Job 14:14

This was Job's question to God.

The Lord Jesus answered Jobs question during His earthly ministry when He said to Martha, *"I am the resurrection, and the life: he that believeth in Me, though he were dead, yet shall he live: And whosoever liveth and believeth in Me shall never die."* John 11:25-26.

Nothing grips our hearts and minds like the loss of a friend or loved one. There is no emptiness like the emptiness left by the Home-going of someone we love.

★ ★ ★ ★ ★   3

God, who is *"the God of all comfort,"* (II Corinthians 1:3) has given us this portion of Scripture to comfort those whose hearts are saddened by the death of their dear loved ones.

God's Word says, *"I would not have you to be ignorant."* The world has always considered God's people to be a little bit ignorant.

But no one is ignorant who knows the One who holds tomorrow, the One who conquered death and the grave.

The Lord Jesus removed the sting of death, and He took the victory away from the grave.

He said, *"I am He that liveth, and was dead; and, behold, I am alive for evermore, Amen; and have the keys of hell and death."* Revelation 1:18

God has some things HE wants us to know about life and death. He gives us these truths to strengthen our hearts in the time of sorrow.

In our comforting text, God speaks to us about three groups of people. He speaks to us *"concerning them which are asleep."* He wants to encourage those of us *"which are alive and remain."* He is very concerned about *"others which have no hope."* He gives great truth to each of these three groups.

Our Comforting Text

"But I would not have you to be ignorant, brethren, concerning them which are asleep, that ye sorrow not, even as others which have no hope. For if we believe that Jesus died and rose again, even so them also which sleep in Jesus will God bring with Him.

For this we say unto you by the word of the Lord, that we which are alive and remain unto the coming of the Lord shall not prevent them which are asleep. For the Lord Himself shall descend from heaven with a shout, with the voice of the archangel, and with the trump of God: and the dead in Christ shall rise first:

Then we which are alive and remain shall be caught up together with them in the clouds, to meet the Lord in the air: and so shall we ever be with the Lord. Wherefore...

Comfort one another with these words. "

I Thessalonians 4:13-18

★ ★ ★ ★ ★   5

"precious in the sight of the LORD is the death of His saints."

Psalm 116:15

Answers About Those Who Have Died

He says, *"But I would not have you to be ignorant, brethren, concerning them which are asleep..."*

First, God is speaking to us concerning those who have died. He is going to tell us about *"them which are asleep,"* those who have died in Christ and have gone Home to be with the Lord.

The Word of God teaches us that *"precious in the sight of the LORD is the death of His saints."* Psalm 116:15

The Lord wants us to have answers about our loved ones who have died. In our comforting text we find answers.

They Are Alive In Heaven

First, God wants us to know that they are still alive. This whole passage speaks of it. They are with the Lord Jesus. God created man *"spirit, soul, and body."* I Thessalonians 5:23. Their body died, but they are still alive.

★ ★ ★ ★ ★   7

Like the beggar who died and was carried by the angels into Abraham's bosom and the thief on the cross whom Christ saved and took to Paradise that day, our friends and loved ones (who die in the Lord) close their eyes in this world and wake up in Glory.

They take their last breath here below and take their next breath in Heaven. They are breathing new air and finding it celestial.

When you die, in Christ, it is not the end of your life. Death is just a door you go through to get to Heaven.

The Bible says, *"For God so loved the world, that He gave His only begotten Son, that whosoever believeth in Him should not perish, but have everlasting life."* John 3:16. Everlasting means everlasting.

When someone puts their faith and trust in the Lord Jesus, as their personal Saviour, the Word of God says they are given eternal life.

The Lord Jesus said, *"My sheep hear My voice, and I know them, and they follow Me. And I give unto them eternal life; and they shall never perish, neither shall any man pluck them out of My hand. My Father, which gave them Me, is greater than all; and no man is able to pluck*

them out of My Father's hand. I and My Father are one."
John 10:27-30.

When Christ said, *"I give unto them eternal life; and they shall never perish,"* He was saying, Do not think that the grave and death are the end.

There is life after death. Life does not end with the death of the body.

The Lord Jesus, when speaking to Martha about her brother who was in the grave, said, *"Thy brother shall rise again."*

Martha replied, *"I know that he shall rise again in the resurrection at the last day."*

Then Jesus told her, *"I am the resurrection, and the life: he that believeth in Me, though he were dead, yet shall he live: And whosoever liveth and believeth in Me shall never die."* John 11:25-26.

The Lord Jesus answered the age-old question, *"If a man die, shall he live again?"* with a glorious *"Yes!"* He taught us that life does not end with death.

The Lord wants us to know that those who have gone on are not buried somewhere in the ground. Their body

★ ★ ★ ★ ★ 9

died and their body is buried, but they did not die. They are with the Lord; they are alive today!

We learn from God's Word that *"the LORD God formed man of the dust of the ground, and breathed into his nostrils the breath of life; and man became a living soul."* Genesis 2:7.

All men one day die: *"Then shall the dust return to the earth as it was: and the spirit shall return unto God who gave it."* Ecclesiastes 12:7.

My dear Mother went Home to be with the Lord over the Thanksgiving holiday in 1999. She is with the Lord this very hour. My beloved "Pop" went Home to be with the Lord eighteen months before my mother did.

I can remember when my son-in-law Tim's grandfather went Home to be with the Lord. Someone asked Tim, "I heard you lost your grandfather?" He said, "No, I didn't lose my grandfather. When you lose something, you do not know where it is. I know where my grandfather is. He is in Heaven."

★ ★ ★ ★ ★

"We are confident, I say, and willing rather to be absent from the body, and to be present with the Lord."

II Corinthians 5:8

Those that are in Heaven are more alive today than they have ever been, and they are presently with the Lord.

They Are With The Lord

The Bible says, *"For if we believe that Jesus died and rose again, even so them also which sleep in Jesus will God bring with Him."* I Thessalonians 4:14.

If the Lord is going to bring them with Him, they must be with Him now. They are with the Lord right now. Is not that wonderful! They are alive, and they are with the Lord.

"Therefore, we are always confident, knowing that, whilst we are at home in the body, we are absent from the Lord: (For we walk by faith, not by sight:) We are confident, I say, and willing rather to be absent from the body, and to be present with the Lord." II Corinthians 5:8.

These are great verses. The Bible says, *"to be absent from the body"* is *"to be present with the Lord."* We are far bet-

★ ★ ★ ★ ★   11

ter off to be absent from the body and to be present with the Lord!

Do you know what happens when a Christian dies? They leave their body, and they are immediately in the presence of God. What a trilling truth!

To *have* His presence in this life is wonderful, but to be in His presence is far better. *"We are confident, I say, and willing rather to be absent from the body, and to be present with the Lord."*

This is why the Apostle Paul said, *"For to me to live is Christ, and die is gain."* Philippians 1:21. How could someone say that *"to die is gain."*

How could someone say it is better to die in Christ than it is to live in Christ? Because to live in His presence is wonderful, but to be in His presence is far better.

The Apostle Paul said he was in a fix. He was torn between two things. He wanted to depart and be with the Lord, but it was more needful, he said, that he remain.

Those who have died in Christ are alive today and are with the Lord. Next, we are given more truth about those who have died.

They Are Living In The Father's House

Not only are they alive today and with the Lord, but also, they are living in the Father's house. How wonderful!

The Lord Jesus said, *"In My Father's house are many mansions...I go to prepare a place for you. And if I go and prepare a place for you, I will come again, and receive you unto Myself; that where I am, there ye may be also."* John 14:2-3.

The Lord Jesus said, *"In My Father's house are many mansions."* People have tried to imagine what those mansions are like.

Heaven is unlike anything we have ever seen or imagined.

Paul said, *"But as it is written, Eye hath not seen, nor ear heard, neither have entered into the heart of man, the things which God hath prepared for them that love Him."* I Corinthians 2:9.

Heaven is going to be so spectacular! What's amazing is that these mansions are in the Father's house. Can you imagine what the Father's house is like?

★ ★ ★ ★ ★ 13

Not only are Christians who have died in Christ alive today, and in the presence of God, but they are also living in the Father's house. Think about that. They are living inside the Father's mansions.

Our Heavenly Home is in a city that is *"the perfection of beauty"* with *"gates...of...pearl"* and a *"street of...pure gold."*

"And the building of the wall of it was of jasper: and the city was pure gold, like unto clear glass. And the foundations of the wall of the city were garnished with all manner of precious stones." Revelation 21:18-19,21.

No wonder Paul said he had a desire to depart and to be with the Lord. Think about our departed loved ones living with Christ in that beautiful place. My dear Pop was a builder. He was very anxious about the new auditorium we built. I was saddened that he went Home to be with the Lord before he could see it completed.

I believe he would have loved it. He was always fascinated with construction. He spoke with me often about special construction projects. I remember when I was a young man, right out of high school, Disney World in Orlando was being built.

People talked about how wonderful it was going to be as they started building that great complex, in central Florida, around the swamps and alligators.

People all over the state of Florida were so excited, waiting until the day it opened. They had to go see it. The first people who went through looked around and said, "Wow! Can you believe this?"

I can remember, as a young man, going through there so amazed at what man had built. My Pop used to talk about those things.

I want you to know that my dear Pop has been with the Lord Jesus and has witnessed the most wonderful building project! He has witnessed the mansions being built. He is living in one today!

Can you imagine what it is going to be like when God takes us to Heaven and reveals His house? Nothing ever built in this world will even come close to what our heavenly Father has built for us.

The Lord is saying, *"I would not have you to be ignorant, brethren, concerning them which are asleep."* They are more alive today than they ever were in this world. And they are in the presence of God.

★ ★ ★ ★ ★

Isn't that wonderful? They are living in the Father's house of many mansions. If we could ask them to come back, they would refuse.

I told our church a while back about a preacher who was on my ordination counsel; Dr. Leroy Perry was an old-fashioned preacher.

Dr. Leroy Perry went home to be with the Lord, and I remember going to his funeral.

About two weeks before Dr. Perry died, the church bought him a brand new fully loaded Buick Park Avenue.

It was some kind of car. One of the preachers who spoke in the funeral service made a comment about it. He said, *"This is a great car. How nice of the church to get it for him. I am sure brother Perry would like to have driven that car a little bit before he went to Heaven."*

Then he thought about what he said, and quickly corrected his statement. He said, *"Pastor Perry has not had one thought about that new car and would not be willing to come back to drive it."*

To be with Christ is far better than anything this world has to offer.

The songwriter had it right when he wrote that the closer we get to Heaven, the more the things of this earth fade away in the *"light of His glory and grace."*

"Precious in the sight of the Lord is the death of his saints."

Psalms 116:15

They Are With Friends And Loved Ones

The Bible says, *"**I** would not have you to be ignorant, brethren, concerning **them** which are asleep."* Who are *"them"*? They are the saints of all the ages who have gone home to be with the Lord. Death for us is a sad good-by to friends and loved ones. But in Heaven it is a grand reunion and welcoming home.

In Heaven there is a wonderful reunion of family and friends. No wonder in Heaven there is *"fullness of joy"* and *"pleasures for evermore."* Psalm 16:11

In Heaven *"there shall be no night."* Revelation 22:5. We will all arrive the same day. In this world we say goodbye, but on the other shore they say hello and welcome home!

★ ★ ★ ★ ★   17

In our sight it is sorrow, but *"precious in the sight of the LORD is the death of His saints."* Psalm 116:15. It is precious because they arrive in a land where there are no more *"tears,"* no more sickness, no more *"pain,"* and no more *"death."* There will be no graves on that bright shore. Revelation 7:17; 21:4; 22:2.

The Lord wants us to know that to be present with Christ is far better than to be in this world. He said, *"concerning them which are asleep,"* they are alive. They are with God. They are in the Father's house, and they are witnessing the building of the mansions.

They are with their friends and loved ones and the saints of all the ages.

The Lord tells us about those who have gone on. They have left this life of pain and sorrow, and now they are in a land where they will never grow old.

"For this cause I bow my knees unto the Father of our Lord Jesus Christ, of whom the whole family in heaven and earth is named, That he would grant you, according to the riches of his glory, to be strengthened with might by his Spirit in the inner man. That Christ may dwell in your hearts by faith."

Ephesians 3:14-17

Next God is going to tell us about those who remain. *"For this we say unto you by the word of the Lord, that we which are alive and remain unto the coming of the Lord shall not prevent them which are asleep."*

★ ★ ★ ★ ★

We must remember in
our sorrow that our life
goes on.

★ ★ ★ ★ ★

Encouragement For Those Who Remain

The Lord wants to help and encourage the families who are *"alive and remain."*

Our Life Must Go On

God tells us not to *"sorrow...as others which have no hope."*

He is not saying that there is no sorrow in the loss of a loved one. The Lord Jesus wept at the grave of Lazarus. His heart was broken, and His eyes were filled with tears. Yet He knew that Lazarus was alive, and He knew where he was.

Truth will not keep your heart from breaking, but it will give you a reason to go on.

It is impossible not to have a broken heart when someone we love and care for dies. However, we must remember in our sorrow that our life goes on. There are

★ ★ ★ ★ ★

others who need us. Our sorrow and heartache is real, but we must not be carried away to where we lose all hope.

Sometimes the survivor of a terrible accident, in which a loved one was taken, has a hard time understanding why they were spared.

When a family member is stricken with sickness, and their life is cut short, we often question, "Why? Why them and not me?"

I came across a poem that was a blessing to me about suffering and death.

Why She Suffered
By O. Ray Burgess

So, you asked me why she suffered
All the days and all the hours,
And I know I cannot tell you.
This lies only in God's powers.
Someday when this life is ended
And the veil of tears has passed,
And we sail into the Harbor
Of God's promises at last,

★ ★ ★ ★ ★

Then we'll know the hidden secrets
He kept back from us a while,
And we'll find our greatest triumph
In the sunshine of God's smile.
In this life we find our trial,
And we suffer through the years,
Often, we are disappointed
And we weep with scalding tears.

But someday when He has called us
To that land of Brighter Day,
We will then be glad we suffered
For it all will pass away.
So, you asked me why she suffered
And I still cannot tell you why,
But we'll know someday, rejoicing,
In that Blessed By and By.

Death cannot take the memory and love we have for people. We are left with precious memories and, in many cases, great lessons of life that can be passed on to the next generation.

The Apostle Paul said, *"I thank my God upon every remembrance of you...because I have you in my heart."* Philippians 1:3,7. Our lives are forever touched and blessed by the people we love and by those who love us.

★ ★ ★ ★ ★

If their life truly influenced our life for good, then we will become their *"crown of rejoicing"* at the Judgment Seat of Christ. I Thessalonians 2:19.

Their influence never ends if we carry their memory with us. They could say, *"For now we live, if ye stand fast in the Lord."* I Thessalonians 3:8.

We Have Something To Look Forward To

The Lord reminds us that when He returns, *"we which are alive and remain shall be caught up together with them in the clouds, to meet the Lord in the air: and so shall we ever be with the Lord."* I Thessalonians 4:17.

He says, *"Weeping may endure for a night, but joy cometh in the morning."* Psalm 30:5. The joy that He is talking about is when we are reunited with our loved ones. We truly have something to look forward to. That "something" is the great resurrection day.

Waiting for a loved one to arrive at the airport, knowing the plane has landed, seeing the passengers start walking toward the waiting area, is exciting.

What joy it is when we see the one we love, and have been waiting for!

Can you imagine the joy we will have when we see the Lord coming in the air with the ones who have gone on before? We have a reason to live, and we have something to look forward to.

We Have Others To Encourage And Help

The Lord said that we should *"comfort one another with these words."* What is hard for us to understand, while we are going through darkness, is that one day our experience of grace will be used to comfort and help others who are going through the same valley.

"Blessed be God, even the Father of our Lord Jesus Christ, the Father of mercies, and the God of all comfort;

"Who comforteth us in all our tribulation, that we may be able to comfort them which are in any trouble, by the comfort wherewith we ourselves are comforted of God." II Corinthians 1:3-4.

We will one day take what we have learned about the grace of God and help others.

Many of our great hymns of faith were written in an hour of sorrow. God draws near to us in these times of heartache and gives us *"in the night His song."* Psalm 42:8.

★ ★ ★ ★ ★ 25

One such song is *It Is Well With My Soul* by H. G. Spafford and Philip P. Bliss.

It Is Well With My Soul

When peace, like a river, attendeth my way,
When sorrows like sea billows roll.
Whatever my lot, Thou has taught me to say,
It is well, it is well with my soul.
And, Lord, haste the day
when my faith shall be sight,
The clouds be rolled back as a scroll,
The trump shall resound
and the Lord shall descend,
"Even-so"--it is well with my soul.

The Lord has left us here to be a blessing and a comfort to others. He will make it possible for our life to cross the path of someone who needs the great truth God has given us, someone for whom we can be a brook by the way.

"Wherefore comfort one another with these words."

★ ★ ★ ★ ★

God Cares For Those Without Hope

The third group we are told about is "***others which have no hope.***" How sad to think of hurting people going through the loss of a friend or loved one and "*having no hope, and without God in the world.*" Ephesians 2:12.

Maybe you are one of those who are without God in this world. To die without hope and without God means to be separated from God forever.

But the Lord cares for you. He wants you to have hope and everlasting life. He tells us in **John 3:16:**

"*For God so love the world, that He gave His only be-gotten Son, that whosoever believeth in Him should not perish, but have everlasting life.*"

The Lord wants you to know that you are **loved**. He said, "*For God so loved the world...*" You are part of this world, and God loves you.

★ ★ ★ ★ ★   27

He also wants you to know that you are of worth. You are so precious to God that *"...He gave His only begotten Son..."* He gave His Son to pay your sin debt.

The Bible teaches us that we are all sinners. *"For all have sinned, and come short of the glory of God."*-**Romans 3:23**. And sin must be paid for. *"For the wages of sin is death..."*-**Romans 6:23**.

The good news is that the Lord Jesus paid our sin debt in full. *"For He hath made Him to be sin for us..."*-**II Corinthians 5:21**. His payment for our sin was accepted by God, and it satisfied God's requirement for forgiveness.

You may ask, *"How can God forgive sin?"* He can do that because of what Jesus did for us. *"...While we were yet sinners, Christ died for us."*-**Romans 5:8**.

God wants you to have **hope**. He said *"...that whosoever believeth in Him should not perish..."* This means that when someone who knows the Lord dies, they are not separated from God. They go to Heaven. The Lord wants all of us to have hope.

God wants you to have a **purpose** in life. He says that we *"should not perish but have everlasting life."*

Everlasting life is ours when we turn to the Lord Jesus Christ in repentance and faith and receive God's payment for our sin. You may ask, "How do I do this?" The answer is as simple as ABC.

- **A**dmit that you are a sinner, *"for all have sinned, and come short of the glory of God."* Romans 3:23.

- **B**elieve that Jesus died for you, for *"Christ died for our sins according to the scripture."* I Corinthians 15:3.

- **C**all upon the Lord to save you, *"for whosoever shall call upon the name of the Lord shall be saved."* Romans 10:13.

Receive Christ today. He has promised, *"Him that cometh to Me I will in no wise cast out."* John 6:37. Come to the Lord Jesus for salvation.

If you would like to know Christ as your personal Saviour and have hope in this world, I invite you to pray this prayer and receive Christ today.

Pray, *"Lord, I know that I am a sinner, and I believe You died and rose again for me. I am trusting You to forgive me. Come into my heart and save me. Help me to live for You. In Jesus' name, Amen."*

★ ★ ★ ★ ★

Everlasting life begins when we receive Christ as our personal Saviour.

*"These things have I written unto you that believe on the name of the Son of God; **that ye may know that ye have eternal life**, and that ye may believe on the name of the Son of God."* I John 5:13.

"Rejoice, because your names are written in heaven."

Luke 10:20

If you have received the Lord Jesus as your personal Saviour, *"there is joy in the presence of the angels of God."* Luke 15:10. Your loved ones in Heaven, at this very moment, are rejoicing over your decision. And you have a great reunion to look forward to.

★ ★ ★ ★ ★

Death Has Been Defeated

Everything about death changed when Jesus rose from the grave. In the Old Testament the Psalmist said, *"Yea, though I walk through the valley of the shadow of death, I will fear no evil: for thou art with me; thy rod and thy staff they comfort me."* Psalm 23:4.

There are no valleys and no shadows in death, for the believer, since Jesus rose from the grave.

Death has been defeated. Jesus said, *"I am he that liveth, and was dead; and, behold, I am alive for evermore, Amen; and have the keys of hell and of death."* Revelation 1:18

There is no fear in death for the child of God. The Bible says in death we are *"absent from the body, and…present with the Lord."* II Corithian 5:8. Jesus said Christians never die. He said to Martha, *"I am the resurrection, and the life: he that believeth in me, though he were dead, yet shall he live: And whosoever liveth and believeth in me shall never die. Believest thou this?"* John 11:25-26

★ ★ ★ ★ ★

Our body dies but we never die. God created man *"spirit and soul and body."* I Thessalonians 5:23

Jesus said we will not even see death. He said to His followers, *"Verily, verily, I say unto you, If a man keep my saying, he shall never see death."* John 8:51. Our body dies, but Christians never die, and they do not see death.

We see our friends and love ones, who die in the faith, close their eyes and leave this world in death. But what we see, they do not see.

We see what happens on the outside because man looks on the outside. But the one dying does not see what we see, they see Jesus. In other words, they leave their body behind in death because God will one day give them a glorious body.

When Stephen was put to death for preaching the Gospel, he said *"Behold, I see the heavens opened, and the Son of man standing on the right hand of God."* Acts 7:56. Stephen did not see his body dying he saw Jesus standing welcoming him home.

When my dear brother left this world in death, he did not see what others around him saw. He saw Jesus standing welcoming him home to Heaven. Heaven is God's gift to believers.

"In my Father's house are many mansions... I go to prepare a place for you...that where I am, there ye may be also."

John 14:2,3

★ ★ ★ ★ ★

Heaven

God's Gift To Believers

There are no shadows in death with Jesus.
There are no valleys we must walk through.
Death is only a doorway,
And all of **Heaven** awaits you.
Our vision on earth is limited -
We see only into the blue,
But in death our vision is endless -
All of Glory comes into view.
Death takes hold of the body,
And our race on earth is through.
The battle for us is over.
With open arms He welcomes you.
So, fear not the end of life's journey.
Believe what God says is true.
Death has been defeated!
Heaven is His gift to you.

★ ★ ★ ★ ★

Keeping Memories Alive

The Bible says, "*For none of us liveth to himself, and no man dieth to himself.*" Romans 14:7. In other words every life has influence, and our influence lives beyond the grave. Some lives leave a positive influence, and some lives leave a negative influence. Every life touches another life, good or bad.

Life Goes On

Life goes on like a flowing river.
Inspiring dreams of love and hope,
Carrying us to the future.

Sometimes roaring,
As it cuts its way through a mountains ridge.
Bringing with it treasures unearthed,
As it flows quietly under a moonlit bridge.

★ ★ ★ ★ ★

Joined by branches,
From many parts' unknown,
Ever winding through the valley,
As life goes on.

Watering seeds planted,
Which seem dead and gone.
Leaving behind new birth,
Awakening nature's resurrection song.

From the headwaters of the world,
Rivers have flowed along.
Touching every life on earth,
As they make their way home.
Arriving at last into the sea,
Joined by other rivers for all eternity.

Moving Forward
After The Loss Of A Loved One

"For to me to live is Christ, and to die is gain."
Philippians 1:21

Moving forward after the loss of a loved one is not easy. There are many areas of one's life that will be altered. People need time to heal.

Guard your heart from becoming bitter.

"Looking diligently lest any man fail of the grace of God; lest any root of bitterness springing up trouble you, and thereby many be defiled." Hebrews 12:15.

The root of bitterness will hinder the future, and every relationship we have with the people we love. We must keep our eyes on Jesus and our heart fixed on Him.

The psalmist said, *"My heart is fixed, O God, my heart is fixed: I will sing and give praise."* Psalm 57:7.

Be careful not to be carried away with sorrow.

"But I would not have you to be ignorant, brethren, concerning them which are asleep, that ye sorrow not, even as others which have no hope." I Thessalians 4:13.

There will be a time of sorrow in the loss of a loved one, but Christians have the promise of being reunited again in Heaven. We have *"hope."*

People who do not know the Lord Jesus, as their personal Saviour, do not have the *"hope"* we Christians hold onto. We know that *"joy cometh in the morning."* Psalm 30:5.

★ ★ ★ ★ ★

That glorious morning is when the Lord Jesus brings with Him our loved ones who are with Him in Heaven.

The Bible says, *"But I would not have you to be ignorant, brethren, concerning them which are asleep, that ye sorrow not, even as others which have no hope. For if we believe that Jesus died and rose again, even so them also which sleep in Jesus will God bring with Him.* I Thessalonians 4:13-14.

Allow the Lord to heal your broken heart.

"He healeth the broken in heart, and bindeth up their wounds." Psalms 147:3.

It is impossible to lose someone you loved and not be brokenhearted. The good news is, the Bible says, *"Blessed be God, even the Father of our Lord Jesus Christ, the Father of mercies, and the God of all comfort."* II Corinthians 1:3. Our God is the God of all comfort.

Other believers are also a source of comfort in this time of sorrow. Our comforting text says, *Wherefore comfort one another with these words."* I Thessalonians 4:13-18. Jesus said, *"as I have loved you, that ye also love one another."* John 13:34.

Share what you have learned with others.

God will allow your path to cross the path of others who will need what you have learned in the valley of sorrow. You will become a treasure and source of strength for others if you allow the Lord to heal you.

"The counsel of the LORD standeth forever, the thoughts of his heart to all generations." Psalm 33:11. Let God use you to help hurting people.

Investing The Influence Of A Person's Life

The influence of our life lives beyond the grave, and will bring our greatest reward, or be the cause of our greatest loss, at the Judgement seat of Christ.

We who are alive and remain have the responsibility of investing the influence of the people we loved and who loved us.

Paul said, *"I thank my God upon every remembrance of you...because I have you in my heart."* Philippians 1:3,7.

I heard a dear lady talk about her favorite uncle. She told about his sense of humor, his fishing stories, his war stories, and a list of other things that captured her imagination when she was a little girl.

★ ★ ★ ★ ★

Her stories about him stirred up an interest in meeting him. I was shocked to discover her favorite uncle had died seventy-five years before she was born. She heard about him, because twice a year the family gathered to decorate the family graves.

The day would be spent telling the next generation stories about their history, and the men and women who had gone on before they were born.

It is a tradition kept by many in the area I grew up in. Sadly, today we hardly have time to get to know all our family, much less talk about the ones who lived a generation before us.

Keeping the memory of our departed loved ones in our heart, and sharing their life story, is the duty of all who remain.

The Story Of Camp Joy

The story of "Camp Joy" will help illustrate this great truth. My beloved pastor, Dr. Lee Roberson and his wife, Caroline, had a baby girl named Joy who died shortly after she was born. They said it was one of the most difficult heartbreaks they faced in all their marriage and ministry.

To keep her memory and influence alive, they began CAMP JOY, a place, "Where boys and girls begin to live."

Over the years thousands upon thousands of boys and girls came to Christ at CAMP JOY.

Dr. Roberson and his sweet wife are in Heaven with their daughter, Joy, today.

They are waiting with all the Christians who have gone on before us, for the great reunion of all of God's children.

They are waiting for the work and influence of their life to be complete. They are waiting for that great crowning day when we stand before our Saviour and give an account of our life and ministry.

★ ★ ★ ★ ★

Joy, who never got to serve the Lord like her brother and sisters, will one day receive a reward for the influence of her life.

Joy's life was lived through CAMP JOY

Even though she never sang a song or taught a Sunday school class, she will receive a reward for her influence. Her influence was invested and managed by her father, mother, and others who kept her memory alive.

The Bible says: *"For none of us liveth to himself, and no man dieth to himself."* Romans 14:7

The story of Camp Joy helped mothers and fathers who lost their children understand that little children who die go to Heaven, and that one day they will be reunited.

David said, concerning his child that died, *"While the child was yet alive, I fasted and wept: for I said, Who can tell whether GOD will be gracious to me, that the child may live? But now he is dead, wherefore should I fast? can I bring him back again? I shall go to him, but he shall not return to me."* II Samuel 12:22-23.

David knew that one day he would die and go to Heaven. He also knew that babies, who die, go to Heaven to be with God. Knowing this great truth gives comfort for those who have suffered the loss of someone they love.

Christians have a glorious reunion to look forward to, when the, *"whole family in heaven and earth,"* is reunited in Heaven. Ephesians 3:15.

Meanwhile, the influence of a lost loved one can motivate others to do a work in memory of their life. The result will be treasures in Heaven.

Think of ways to invest the influence of your loved one. I wrote a poem to help remind family and friends of the wonderful people who invested their life in us.

The poem "You Were On My Heart Today," is a reminder that Christians will one day be reunited together in Heaven with their friends and loved ones.

May we all have a good day when we see Jesus.

★ ★ ★ ★ ★

You Were On My Heart Today

As I read again of that crowning day,
When face to face we will meet,
In our Heavenly home, with golden streets.
You could not come back to me,
But I will soon come to you,
There was much together, we did do.
Before Christ we will one day stand,
And receive our reward for following His plan.
Work was done in memory of you.
It was because of your loss, that I stayed true.
Through salvation so many are made free.
Because you continued to live,
You lived through me.

★ ★ ★ ★ ★

Remembering Your Loved One

"I thank my God upon every remembrance of you…because I have you in my heart."

Philippians 13,7

The following pages are dedicated to record your fond memories, and lessons of life, to share with future generations.

Remebering _____ Date _____

_____

_____

_____

_____

_____

_____

_____

_____

_____

_____

_____

_____

_____

_____

_____

_____

_____

_____

_____

_____

_____

_____

_____

_____

_____

_____

_____

_____

_____

_____

_____

_____

_____

_____

_____

_____

_____

_____

★ ★ ★ ★ ★

All Scripture taken from the Authorized Version

1. I Thessalonians 4:13-18
2. Job 14:14
3. John 11:25-26
4. II Corinthians 1:3
5. I Corinthians 15:55-57
6. Revelation1:18
7. Psalm 116:15
8. I Thessalonians 5:23
9. Luke 16:22
10. Luke 23:43
11. John 10:9
12. John 10:27-30
13. John 11:23-26
14. Genesis 2:7
15. Ecclesiastes 12:7
16. II Corinthians 5:6-8
17. Philippians 1:21
18. Philippians 1:23-24
19. John 14:2-3
20. I Corinthians 2:9
21. Psalm 50:2
22. Revelation 21:21
23. Revelation 21:18-19
24. Helen Howarth Lemmel, "Turn Your Eyes Upon Jesus"
25. Psalm 16:11
26. Revelation 21:25; 22:5
27. Psalm 116:15
28. Revelation 7:17; 21:4; 22:2; Isaiah 25:8; I Corinthians 15:26
29. John 11:35
30. O. Ray Burgess, By Still Waters, 1949
31. Philippians 1:3, 7
32. I Thessalonians 2:19
33. I Thessalonians 3:8
34. Psalm 30:5
35. II Corinthians 1:3-4
36. Psalm 42:8
37. Ephesians 2:12
38. Romans 3:23
39. I Corinthians 15:3
40. Romans 10:9-13
41. John 6:37
42. I John 5:13
43. Luke 15:10

WordToTheWorld@aol.com

www.FiveStarChristianMinistries.com

www.ingramcontent.com/pod-product-compliance
Lightning Source LLC
Chambersburg PA
CBHW051245120626
46547CB00014B/1806